SUN BEAR

BOOKS BY MATTHEW ZAPRUDER

POETRY

Sun Bear
Come On All You Ghosts
For You in Full Bloom (with Chris Uphues)
The Pajamaist
American Linden

TRANSLATION

Secret Weapon: Selected Late Poems of Eugen Jebeleanu
(with Radu Ioanid)

SUN BEAR

MATTHEW ZAPRUDER

For Dan –

thanks! all the best

COPPER CANYON PRESS

PORT TOWNSEND, WASHINGTON

Copper Canyon Press is in residence at Fort Worden State Park in Port Townsend, Washington, under the auspices of Centrum. Centrum is a gathering place for artists and creative thinkers from around the world, students of all ages and backgrounds, and audiences seeking extraordinary cultural enrichment.

LIBRARY OF CONGRESS CATALOGING-IN-PUBLICATION DATA
Zapruder, Matthew, 1967–
  [Poems. Selections]
  Sun bear / Matthew Zapruder.
      page cm.
  ISBN 978-1-55659-463-2 (PBK.)
  I. Title.

  PS3626.A67S86 2014
  811'.6—DC23
                              2013033258
                98765432 FIRST PRINTING

Copper Canyon Press
Post Office Box 271
Port Townsend, Washington 98368
www.coppercanyonpress.org

ACKNOWLEDGMENTS

Immense thanks to the editors of the following publications, where the poems in this book first appeared, sometimes in different forms:

Alaska Quarterly Review, American Poet, Arc, Bat City Review, The Believer, Berkeley Poetry Review, Blackbird, Boston Review, California Northern, Event, Explosion-Proof, Floating Wolf Quarterly, Guernica, Gwarlingo, The Harvard Advocate, Jai Alai, The Laurel Review, Likestarlings, Los Angeles Review of Books, Magnitude, Map Literary, The Massachusetts Review, The Moment, Narrative, Occupy Writers, On and On Screen, The Paris-American, PEN Poetry Series, *Plume,* Poem-A-Day (Academy of American Poets), *Poetry, Poetry International, Poetry London, A Public Space, The Rattling Wall, Real Simple, Route 9, Telephone, Tin House, T: The New York Times Style Magazine, Tuesday, Two Weeks, The Walrus.*

I'm very grateful as well to the editors at *The Rumpus* for including me in *Letters in the Mail,* as well as to the editors of *The Best American Poetry 2013* for reprinting "Albert Einstein," which first appeared in *The Believer.* I'd also like to thank the editors of the anthology *The Book of Scented Things,* who sent me a small mysterious unlabeled vial of what turned out to be Philosykos by Diptyque. Its "wooded and racy nourishing accents" of fig, cedar, and longing inspired the writing of "Poem for a Vial of Nameless Perfume."

Special thanks also to Lannan Foundation and the John Simon Guggenheim Memorial Foundation.

for Sarah

CONTENTS

I

II

III

SUN BEAR

I

Sun Bear

yesterday at the Oakland zoo
I was walking alone for a moment
past the enclosure holding the sun bear
also known as *beruang madu*
it looked at me without interest
it has powerful jaws and truly loves honey
it sleeps in a high hammock
its claws look made out of wood
and if it dreams at all it is of Malaysia
home of its enemy the clouded leopard
a gorgeous arboreal
hunting and eating machine
whose coat resembles a python
now it is night and the zoo is closed
some animals are sleeping
the nocturnals moving in their cages
getting ready to hunt nothing
I don't know why but I feel sure
something has woken the sun bear
it is awake in the dark
maybe it is my spirit animal
I am reading about the early snow
that has fallen on the Northeast
all the power shutting down
the weather going insane
the animals cannot help us
they go on moving without love
though we look into their eyes and feel
sure we see it there and maybe
we are right nothing

can replace animal love
not even complicated human love
we sometimes choose to allow
ourselves to be chosen by
despite what everyone knows
the problem is
in order to love anything
but an animal you cannot allow
yourself to believe in those things
that are if we don't stop them
going to destroy us

Aubergine

I lie in bed
staring at the ceiling
last night before
I fell asleep
I put the book
on the floor
looking down
I see its spine
with the golden
simple name
of the old
poet who might
already be dead
somehow he used
ancient magic
everyone says
we don't need anymore
to place inside
me that perfect
sadness
at last
after all the formal
words of love
I could really imagine
how terrible
some day
not for fifty
years or so
but still
for one of us

to say goodbye
it will be
again fear
that is almost
seasickness and also
surely irrational
hope by that time
I will in some
way feel "ready"
through me
moves and then
asleep again
I am wearing
a dead rich
man's black
luxurious overcoat
gold buttons
it is snowing
in a vast
wooden hallway
I am not cold
someone laughing
says just watch
them learn the same
lessons he means
my children I don't
have yet
I touch the head
of a very important
black goat
and wake up again
the clock radio

says a small
tremor shook
some part
of the desert
no one lives in
tiny drones
we are flown
by what we do
not know into
blue election
season
inevitable spells
are cast
by warlocks
they move
their hands
and factories
rise or stadiums
into dust
collapse
8:10 a.m. December
San Francisco
rainy season
you pull on
your boots
I call them purple
the label says
Aubergine
you leave
for work
and by a jolt
of atavistic

sadness electrified
I move
once again
to the impassive
black desk
to clock
in for my eternal
internship
at the venerable
multinational
not for profit
Lucid & Dreaming

What Can Poetry Do

In Africa people are angry.
They are climbing embassy walls
and burning whatever is there.
Each time I click on some words
and read what we call news
I feel certain some people
while I was reading have died.
I know I am here merely reading.
I just sit in my room and worry.
As always I can do nothing.
So I close all the portals and go
deep in my mind to discover
something about Tunisia.
Tunisia of desert silence
broken by occasional battles
where a man set himself on fire
then revolution then elections.
Tunisia whose cosmopolitan
capital city Carthage
the Romans completely destroyed.
Tunisia where they filmed
the familiar home planet scenes
of the space movie we all stood in line
a million years ago to see.
I don't know anything else.
Now I remember something
I once read about the forests
people are carefully growing
far from the capital city.
The trees are eating the poison

probably much too slowly.
But still they take the particles
and even if we don't deserve it
our air is a little clearer.
It's like the painting I saw
of a witch in the forest
her hair in a black column rising
like smoke from a burning structure.
She was dragging three or four ropes
the color of umbilical blood.
She was guarded by her wolf familiar.
At first she terrified me.
Then I saw she was causing
certain spells to protect
far away new mothers
whose children must in the middle
of great violence be born.
The men surround the embassy.
It will never be clear who sent them.
For a moment I feel ashamed.
I breathe the clear terrible air.

Public Art

I hate bees E. said
holding a spoon
and I thought how zen
to admit it
for without
those mechanical golden
creepers moving
among the crops
with powder
on their wings
unbeknownst
we would
be super fucked
they are
said G. refusing
a small ceramic
cup of wine
necessary
and therefore good
even that one
stuck in the lamp
will just go to sleep
when you do
we could see
part of her face
frown slightly
then smile remembering
how good it will be
to be awakened
at that hour

only trucks
move in the streets
M. watched it
crawl furiously along
the intricate white
tubing of one
of those new bulbs
we all are addicted
to light he said
and it is just one
of ten thousand
husbands
then S. said
do you think its feet
hurt and I was
suddenly aware
of my toe
she is my only
husband and I
her only flower
of many changing
colors that every
morning grows
up through the black
soil of what is not
into the early
light that reflects
at least a little
color off
whichever dress
I help her choose

How Do You Like the Underworld

The completely to me magical screen
sits in the middle of this black desk
I put together with such trouble,
following the instructions, muttering
its nonsensical Swedish name like a spell.
The screen is a dark window.
It can be made slowly light
by pushing a single button. It nobly rises,
a monument to a process begun
some years ago in a completely
dust free facility thousands of miles
from Oakland where the free sun
beats gently down on the heads
of my neighbors. I hear them
now for two sunlit moments pause
to converse as their dogs touch noses.
Meanwhile in the factory the workers
wear white dustproof suits.
The boss watches from a catwalk above.
To be troubled only abstractly
by the thought the thought in me
of those totally pure white clad
very real workers makes me
a kind of boss
though I wish I were not
is the ultimate white person problem.
To solve it I would like to ask
an ancient philosopher, preferably one in a cave.
But they are extinct. The humans
who are not robots at all

are right now robotically putting together
insanely precise atomic components
that make what we do go.
Thus I can watch and interact
with people I call followers or friends.
Or rather the words they have put together.
Down the screen they scroll.
It makes me so dizzy.
For a while I watched and thought
how interesting. Then sad
thinking animals. Without a thought
to make them close
I closed my eyes and saw
a monk reading a book in the garden.
The book was about music others
left for us long ago and departed.
What can you learn
from a book about music?
Some say to settle for winter.
But they have read way too much Rilke,
he is very dead, and his problems
though cosmic did not include
the round earth becoming hotter.
I heard somewhere in Africa
they have found a glittering valley
an asteroid crashed into millions of years ago
and filled with useful silicate.
The frustules i.e. shells of single cell
diatoms, make a white earth
you can pack into tiny packets
to keep things dry on their journeys
to our stores. I bought some

at Grand Lake Ace Hardware to combat
the tiny harmless ants that plagued me.
They plague me no more.
It's time for the patriots to move forward.
Let's go live now to that lake.
The smooth black totally ichthyic
divers plunge. To watch them
and wonder is like donning
the ceremonial oven mitts and trying
to grab a black coin in a darkened basement.
Beautiful pre-middle-aged people,
right now in the uncountable moments
interposed between us and lunch
together we sleepwalk
in the best interest of claws.
We have broken the future of thunder.
Is it interesting or sad? There is no difference.
All children's books are now about death.

Poem without Intimacy

the other day I was shopping

in one of those giant incredibly brightly lit stores

you can apparently see from space

wheeling a massive empty cart

thinking this is a lot like thinking

why do I go to sleep

not having brushed my teeth and dream

of the giant failure

known as high school again

on the loudspeaker was a familiar song

by Quicksilver Messenger Service

there were no lyrics but I remember

it says we are all skyscrapers

under one blue rectangle

that never chose us

to be these sentinels

who imperceptibly sway

and watch people far below

like tiny devices no one controls

enter our various sunlit glass conversations

the world is old

and full as it will always be

of commerce and its hopeful nonprofit mitigations

future products from the Amazon

will cure ailments we have

and also ones not yet invented

looking down I saw my cart was full

of a few boxes of some cereal I do not recognize

four flashlights and a pink plastic water bottle

made of some kind of vegetable

that will eventually like me into the earth

harmlessly decompose

and then I passed an entire row of plastic flowers

and wanted to be the sort of person

who bought them all

but really I am a runway covered in grass

and all I truly love is sleep

My Childhood

the orange ball arcs perfectly into the orange hoop

making a sound like a drawer closing

you will never get to hold that

I am here and nothing terrible will ever happen

across the street the giant white house full of kids

turns the pages of an endless book

the mother comes home and finds the child animal sleeping

I left my notebook beside the bed

the father came home and sat and quietly talked

one square of light on the wall waiting patiently

I will learn my multiplication tables

while the woman in the old photograph looks in a different direction

Poem for England

I prefer the old translations
sometimes instead of the printed words
I am by small blue stars
and sentences she wrote
earnestly many years ago
in pen in the margins
distracted
now I touch
this same book she carried
under her arm or in a bag
up some steps and sat down
in the library and worried
something extremely important
would happen or not
and now I have taken it
down from the shelf
and when some god
speaks winged elaborate
phrases though I am modern
it feels necessary to me
hello England are you there
I said into the plastic telephone
one of those old ones
I bought at a tag sale
the sound pulses somehow
used to run
through a long plastic cord
attached to the wall
moving the tiny ear bones
in Massachusetts where the Pilgrims

landed one summer
England we think
we are modern our language
some kind of harmful
blue green despair fire
covering the globe
some very new galaxy
everyone else is watching
through telescopes our altruistic scientists
invented but really
we are very old
and you are young
you are our very old baby
we are pretending to neglect
for your own good
it has grown darker
let us turn back to the book
now we are just touching its pages
everyone in it died a long time ago
trying to get home

Poem for Engagement

Even though
every morning
I remember
I'm so glad
the day begins
we go on
it's our secret
you and I know
who can know
this afternoon
no one stares
from the windows
the alley
is empty
strange to think
the spaces
will be filled by dreaming
people thinking
they're awake
we are people
and we know
how real a dream
when it's empty
but for the few
great questions is

Poem for a Persian Singer

when I held the envelope

full of music

my friend had sent

I knew the time

a little harmless

loneliness would guide

my hand holding

the circular polycarbonate

plastic disc

with the blue letters

spelling her name

into the machine

had come

and I heard

her voice inside me

make deep

ancient canyons

only sunlight

has ever known

some time passes

I suddenly notice

it is afternoon

I am standing

in the kitchen

holding a broom

she stops singing

alone for a while

the music wanders

then her voice returns

she says a word

it sounds like *glacier*

I'm pretty sure ·

the song describes

how it feels when

something important

does not happen

most of the afternoon

still listening I think

beautiful old stove

many people

we will never know

placed their hands

on your dials

hoping things

would never change

I cannot imagine

what it is like

for those who know

they must stand together

thinking for too long

we have waited

for fear which is not

a guest to leave

they might shoot us

but we will stay

here in the street

until we are all

at last older sisters

to each other

Poem for Giants

for months we have been walking
sometimes with earbuds in our ears
listening to the voice of Jon Miller
tell us what is happening this afternoon
to our little Giants on the green
and also brown with white chalk
fields of San Diego Cincinnati or St. Louis
each park with its own parameters
I remember hearing his voice
on my clock radio almost every night
the summer of 1983 as the Baltimore Orioles
moved inexorably toward their destiny
it was very hot and I was learning to drive
and sometimes there are longer silences
and for a few seconds we start thinking
about work or our relationships
and then someone shifts from one position
to another and there is a lot to say
not about the anger that lately
has been the only thing bringing people
closer together or the voting
already happening in many states
and a small crowd parts for an ambulance
to back up and bring a little bed
on wheels closer to someone who has fallen
and is now sitting up already breathing
a little easier and saying no no I don't
want to go but they take him anyway
there is a light rain on everything
on some faces there is the hint of orange

from the brims of caps we feel happy
to feel a little silly about wearing
these are as they say difficult times
but maybe all that means is we are changing

Poem for Japan

all day staying inside

listening to a podcast

discuss how particles

over the Pacific

might drift

I knew thinking

whenever *cloud*

scares me

I am not alone

my umbrella slept

in the closet

I placed a few nouns

in beautiful cages

then let them out

touched with my mind

the lucky cat

asleep in the deli

I always scratch

his head he slightly

raises to meet my hand

all over the remains

contaminated shadowmen

in blue suits that seem

ecclesiastical now

that science is

a religion crawl

the emperor

everyone has forgotten

is speaking

no one knows

how to be

loving and also

hope the wind

in a certain

and not another

direction will blow

The Moment

at certain moments I lift my head

and remember my backyard

which is not really mine

but I have paid rent

so I get to look at it here

in the most touristy neighborhood

of this sleepy city San Francisco

connected to everything by bridges

so maps make it look from above

like a lopsided starfish

I always forget how close I live to the water

and in those moments I manage

to become incrementally less

than fully distracted by obligations

I cannot even remember

I reach my hand

up to open the venetian blinds

and usually see not much happening

maybe a crow pecking

at one of the plants in rows

the gardener my landlord

has hired to create

vegetables out of nothing

but soil and seeds and water

and whatever music

she listens to through her headphones

sometimes I see her do a funny dance

right before she turns on the hose

or a small mouse running

furiously to the old blue chair

where it's safe and shadowy

and I know in just a few months

I will get married

underneath a tree whose leaves

say beautiful worried lovers

no matter what anyone says to you

when we rustle we are saying believe us

though we know you know leaves don't speak

and I also know some day

or maybe it has already passed

there will be one

I won't even notice when I am halfway

through everything I will do

and I will have started

to wear my body like an old machine

that wants nothing not even

the long gone intimation of celerity

or something else that cannot be recalled

II

A Benefit Celebration for Copper Canyon Press

Featuring Matthew Zapruder

Hosted by Bill and Ruth True

May 28, 2014

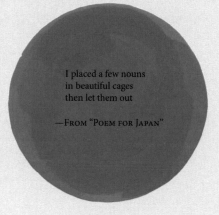

I placed a few nouns
in beautiful cages
then let them out

—From "Poem for Japan"

7:00 Reception
7:30 Welcome and Dinner
A Reading and Conversation
with Matthew Zapruder
8:00 An Appeal for Poetry

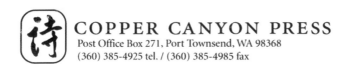

COPPER CANYON PRESS

Post Office Box 271, Port Townsend, WA 98368
(360) 385-4925 tel. / (360) 385-4985 fax

Yes! I/we would like to sustain the mission of Copper Canyon Press.

Name(s): _____

Date: _____

My/Our donation is $ _____ per year for _____ years.

_____
Signature

Preferred Method of Contact:

Phone_____

Email_____

Please list me/us in the following way for donor recognition:

_____

Thank you for your support of Copper Canyon Press.

Korea

It is very early
the apartment is cold

Sarah is still asleep
I ask myself

if I am not
a garbageman

why am I
awake in the world

I guess to the side
of the large

rattling green
truck sized worry

gathering all these
beautiful theories

and feelings
to cling

when the sky
gets lighter

I will try
in my desk chair

to sort them
when I first

turned on the light
I saw a fruit fly

orbiting nothing
above the sink

so like I read
in some magazine

I filled two plastic
containers with

a little vinegar
and poked holes

in saran wrap
to catch it before

like last summer
it finds another

and breeds
for weeks laughing

and angry
we chased them

around the apartment
eager to amputate

what was if one
can call it that

their dream to live
with their ten

thousand children
in a mango

or bagel that rolled
behind the refrigerator

for hours I sit
in the kitchen

and watch the traps
on the radio I hear

a solemn voice
repeat war games

in the Yellow Sea
on a map with my finger

I trace the kingdom
of Korea

it looks like a blue
friendly seahorse

ready for gentle
locomotion

hello Lord
sorry I woke you

because my plans
are important to me

and I need things
no one can buy

and don't even know
what they are

I know I belong
in this new dark age

Poem for Wine

I don't drink wine

much anymore

though I love that not

feeling feeling

of not remembering

having pressed

the giant translucent

anxious button

in my chest

that turns

something I don't

know the name of

off and a pure wise

hilarity vector among

the conversation clusters

I float bestowing

my sometimes speaking

at others just silently

sparkling full of potential

energy presence

and later I remember

I have always been

an exiled prince

who could but has not

chosen yet to return

to govern my fully

adoring people

I've also never

taken Ecstasy

then sat on a couch

in Peru 14%

excited licking

a hot person

dressed like a rabbit

I do remember

analog porn

somehow holding

an inevitable magazine

always feeling

without knowing

how to say it

true ecstasy

would be to stand

above myself protecting

me as I turn

those sudden blessed

horrible corners

Poem for Plutocrats

One mild day
the body walks
out of the lobby
made of glass
then past blue tents
and all the shouting
people he thinks
cannot or refuse
to see abstractions
like money and rights
must be delicately
assembled into
great forces
no one can touch
so those forces
in turn will push
machinery that wants
nothing not even
to stay still
into building
a factory or bridge
these people
can work in or cross
he thinks
what they do not
understand
is whatever is
must exactly
be this way
no matter what

nothing will change
we will always
be selfish
and now it has
begun to rain
the body gets
a little warmer
soon it will
lie in bed
and the doctors
will solemnly rush
to the bedside
and do many things
tiny silver
containers will be
placed inside
the body to hold
terrible radiation
next to whatever
must be eradicated
but everyone
will know it is
the end some say
is just another
country to be ruled
and maybe many
years from now
long after the body
has gone back
into the earth
where it belongs
young people

talking and laughing
will move
through a door
below his name
carved in gold
into a room
and sit down to learn
gentle techniques
for bringing justice
to others
and ourselves
discovered at last
by people
all of us
alive today
are much too old
to know

I Drink Bronze Light

Great American summer lakes
right now I am flying above you
through a rare cloudless transparent sky
back to the city where it is always
cold even in summer
the round hole I press my face against
shows only a blue expanse
with white sails below
speckled exactly the way
the Aegean would have been
three thousand years ago
if one could have seen it from above
maybe riding in the dark claw
of a god who didn't care
through the round window
weird white light
bounces off the cubes in my glass
of clear diet soda that tastes
completely theoretical
huge blue lake I do not know
which one you are
maybe Superior I can't see land
on either side and for a moment
feel I have just woken up
to wonder if there is an ocean
I have forgotten along our route
now I see some giant black
thunderclouds we are steering
away from and I wish I were
on the ground in the seaside town

we are now flying over
named for a general
in the French and Indian Wars
for a moment it seems
someday she and I will choose
to spend a summer there
swimming every day
then buying some ice cream
and walking the faded blue boards
back into town where evening
awaits us holding fireflies
and a low barely perceptible
air conditioner hum
when it gets dark we will go
our skin still hot with radiation
to the new restaurant
and calmly discuss the election
things are going to get better
our wise choices fill us with peace
not to mention cake and such
a particular love like the one
I have for the green scrunchie
in her hair and the t-shirt
with the mermaid she wears
only when we go to sleep
I will be with her for a long time
because unlike Columbus
lying to his men about how far
they had gone and who first saw
light on the new continent
to all new things I discover
I mean no harm and do not

even secretly believe
anything I find on our journey
will make me live forever

Poem for Engagement

when they left we were not so sad
and everything continued
a little question inside us asking
where did those young ones
and their baby blue egg

the nest is empty
the wind shaking it
and lately we have to the grocery store
been walking thinking yes
I silently agree
everyone worships us
because we have declared our love

they think we have stood before the Parthenon
and silently pondered
the philosophical questions
actually we were talking a lot
about what we just had for lunch
and arguing why some wine is green

green wine like the ocean
would taste if it weren't full of salt
each day I drink a mouthful
my own life my secret mountain
I am never going to climb

I am going to tell you
something incredibly useful
to remember next month
when I am flying over Omaha

and you are in bed listening
to what is not there

though I know no one
in that city it will for a moment
seem to me as if I am going to meet
a friend who will say a true decision
is one you do not understand

It Is Tuesday

From room to room

after you left

I wandered a while

in the hours

I have cooked

the mushroom soup

as instructed

picked up a paperback

I once read

but forgot

had some coffee

it is quiet

I don't know why

all afternoon

I think of you

in the traffic

the rain

peacefully falling

like some plastic beads

from the '70s

when they took all the doors

off the closets

and our parents smoked

all night downstairs

and laughed too loud

we couldn't hear

what they were

and what they knew

if you hate me

it must be

for ancient reasons

Your Eyes Are the Color of a Lightbulb Floating in the Potomac River

Just when it is time to say goodbye

I think I am finally understanding the lightbulb

but not milk or NAFTA or for that matter paper money

let's not get into my stove top coffeemaker

I don't even get how this book is fastened or why that orchid

seems happier or at least its petals a little whiter

when it is placed right up against the window

or how certain invisible particles

leave the wall and enter the cord and somehow make

the radio make the air become

Moonlight Sonata or Neighborhood #3

basically a lamp is a mechanism

to shove too many electrons into a coil

or filament a lightbulb i.e. a vacuum surrounds

the first filament was made in 1802 out of platinum

as soon as it was made to turn deep untouchable orange

the air took the electrons away

which left it charred like a tiny bonfire

just like ones we have all seen when we squint and hold

the glass bulb that no longer emits

soft white light when we flip the switch

I wonder if my fear this morning sitting in the dark

and listening to music is anything like

the inventor of the telephone growing deaf

and knowing all those poles and wires

were starting to cover the land and someday everyone

would be able to get exactly what they want

Poem for Wisconsin

In Milwaukee it is snowing

on the golden statue

of the 1970s television star

whose television house

was in Milwaukee

and also on the Comet Cafe

and on the white museum

the famous Spanish architect

built with a glass

elevator through it

and a room with a button

that when you press it

makes two wings

on the sides of the building

more quickly than you might

imagine mechanically

rise like a clumsy

thoughtful bird

thinking now I am

ready at last

to fly over the lake

that has many moods

but it will not

and people ask

who are we who see

so much evil and try

to stop it and fail

and know we are no longer

for no reason worrying

the terrible governors

are evil or maybe

just mistaken and nothing

can stop them not even

the workers who keep

working even when

it snows on their heads

and on the bridge

that keeps our cars

above the water

for an hour

in northern California

today it snowed

and something

happened people

turned their beautiful

sparkling angry faces up

Poem for a Coin

strange coin I would call bronze
on what feels like earth's last morning
I stand in the kitchen just holding
your slight warmth in my palm
trying now to remember
from what country I removed you
maybe Slovenia or terrible Spain
you clink against the gold
I wear on the finger known as ring
on one side a number on the other
some famous candelabra
a solemn crowd once a year
along the main avenue carried
to celebrate Night the considerate guest
that while we are sleeping quietly
takes its clouds and departs
or a shield that long ago
protected a prince from an arrow
so he could become the cruel
organizer whose roads to this day
we still unthinking travel
strange coin I am asking
whose hands without marveling
held you on their way
though you know you cannot answer
some mornings I wander out
below the sun scare some crows
grab a spade and make a hole
place some seeds or a whole plant
my wife tells me what to do

she is holding an orange can
full of clear miraculous water
her dark hair her white skin
after a funeral I have seen
loved ones ritually pound
dirt with shovels to make
the rectangular hole flat and ready
for the stone we will return to
so many years each time to place
atop it some small object from the world
for some reason we cannot explain
maybe to wish the souls
we don't know if we believe in
safe journey to nowhere
just in case wherever they are
they will know they are
thought of and remembered

Poem to a Cloud above a Statue

Out of what used to be called the aether

very powerful beings

ancient people believed

they knew the names of

breathed instead of air

but now we just call the sky

you came

not really looking like anything

or maybe a little bit like if you could talk

you would choose silence as a subject

and I felt completely sure

you would never ask me

to think about the past

except maybe those days I will confess

even though it is silly I still think of as holy

a few of us used to meet at The Gate

for what we called a drink

but as you know truly were many

living on Eastern Parkway

against not being made

to do anything I leaned

and leaning was my secret tombstone

with soft grass all around it

I fell asleep many times in the sun

through the window and thought

I will never wake up

but I didn't die I moved to California

where I see you cloud

and want to tell you this is the last time

I will ever arrive in a new place a stranger

expecting to be welcomed

then tenderly ignored

and now you are suddenly a giant tree!

solemnly laughing beside a terrifying river

no one has ever stepped into

Poem for Massachusetts

these days
sometimes you sleep

in a purple t-shirt
that says Massachusetts

which means something
in an older language

I can never remember
for one whole year

before I knew you
driving down Route 9

thinking nothing
seemed so hard

I just kept singing
stay with the plan

each time it felt wronger
which is a word

adults pretending
to pretend

to be childlike use
I heard it one

time when the leaves
in a drawing

someone I don't
know anymore

handed to me
were blue it was

how sick she was
I should have known

her long fingers
shook all summer

green chlorophyll
covers up the colors

all the tourists
in the fall

later come to see
I can't tell you

how many people
in the making

of the experience
that made this poem

were harmed
sometimes leaves

are an emblem
meaning an object

symbolizing something
abstract like glory

or destruction
and sometimes

just sunlight
delivery systems

To Sergio Franchi

Listening to you sing Stella by Starlight I am thinking of the hummingbird
I actually see almost every morning hovering in the garden

I think it has a green chest but it moves too fast to really be sure
It seems to particularly love those purple flowers

Whose names no matter how many times I am told I cannot remember
Sergio Franchi I am giving in to spending a long slow hour

Holding a book closed in my lap and reading about your life
As a youth you studied both music and engineering

I imagine in those days you were not entirely happy
It makes sense later you would be so fearless

Staring into the very hot lights on the stage of the Ed Sullivan show
With effortless force pushing the air

That made the sound so beautiful and rending
My heart and I for once agree

At that moment not unlike a laundromat at night
Your light is so artificial it truly seems too real

And with a little sweat forming on your very sculptural forehead it is clear
Even you know you could never prepare us for even one long terrible afternoon

Yesterday I was walking down Stockton avoiding the many pedestrians
Crowded around the Chinese groceries with their marvelous enigmatic produce

I was feeling a little rage and also some happiness when a small gray cat
Who might or might not have been lost came up to me and with his forehead
      bumped my shin

Great singer, forgive me
Being myself has been a welcome unconscious chore

Today when I pass a person on the street I promise to think
You there, you could be a beautiful singer

I have carried several problems here and would like to leave them
But then who would I be

Poem for Americans

When I go to the bank
California mild afternoon
fills my frame
hollow with desire
to formally say
American brothers and sisters
let us look up
from our screens.
Toward my numbers
I walk, a tragic
precursor condemned
to an easy life
balanced on the suffering
in another land
of strangers I might
someday speak to
when I call to complain.
Inside the low beige
building I tap
my not really secret
code and the machine
takes the paper
into this very real
legal fiction I will die
without understanding.
I pass an old man
carrying a package
and feel suddenly
sure he is of something
a great master.

He looks like the dignified
slow moving born
during the last great war
people I passed
that summer in Paris
I felt so important
and proud to suffer.
On the television our president
has just finished speaking.
Soon it will be winter
and my childhood anxious
home in Maryland
through its windows
onto the street will glow.
I will go there
and touch the banister
I threw a small wooden
turtle my sister
loved over then sleep
in the room
where I learned
to be so angry.
All night Norse gods
and white polar foxes
run out of the large
green book I read
every night
as if those stories
far away people
told could put
some order to mine.
In the morning I plunge

my hand into
the cigar box I threw
all my quarters into.
In my pocket I put
a heavy silver handful.
You never know when
you might see
an expiring meter.
The American lie is you
and the man wearing
the uniform can agree.
Americans when he comes
to your door ignore
the faint bell.
Your desire to pay
what you owe
touches many things.
Like a husband
blowing out some candles
battle it in the darkness.

III

Poem for Happiness

the dead spider rested on my windowsill
using one piece of paper I pushed it

onto another piece of paper
then dropped it accidentally

behind some old paint cans next to the door
the orange tulips you gave me

for a second seemed to be in a mostly nice way
laughing as I bent down

wearing dishwashing gloves a blue
color not found in nature

in order to find the little brown body
that was for primal reasons

horrifying me and stand in the doorway
and hold it out in front of me

to the wind which even if everywhere else
in the city it is calm

rushes down our street
where the yellow Kawasaki is always

parked next to the green bin
I threw the candles we can't light anymore

into because their wicks are gone
and you cried because

I had thrown out the beautiful candles
the sun turns in a different direction

everything becomes suddenly chrome
and now I am thinking on a hillside

where the wind is blowing very strongly
we will get married

our future a long sunny avenue
we have already walked partway down

or a pink umbrella
or a very loud water feature

in the middle of the city
around it on a concrete ledge

the workers sit next to each other
even though they do not know each other

and read silently together and alone

The Heart Is Not a Door

when the very old cat leaps from the last wooden stair
to the floor her left knee buckles
somehow gracefully she rises

already dispassionately into the distance
staring then limping off into the bedroom
all day she sleeps

her masters absent
helpless we are doing nothing watching her
hoping she lives through the weekend

and also realizing why people have things
it is very comfortable we also understand
exactly why they call steel stainless

the coffeemaker senses light and begins
making just enough noise so we notice
how quietly everything here in the suburbs

has landed exactly where it should
beige art on the walls
represents the space in my head my bare feet

through the luscious fibers of the carpet move
I stop at the screen door and stare
into the infinity pool whose waters

pour over the edges and flow
a green hose again makes the same arc
a whip striking clear blue water

I should go for a swim it's my only chance
to hold my breath and open my eyes
later I drink some green wine then splash

some in the pan I am frying sweet multicolored peppers
when they get soft I toss them
with intricate curled pasta

I don't know the name of and oil
pressed by hand from olives someone plucked
from old trees still growing

over the tomb of the twin founders of Rome
as they have for thousands of years
or so says the bottle

I have now been staring at for at least several minutes
later I slip a blade into the razor
to feel cleaner but I don't

my face stares back you grew up
in this sort of house exactly
part of the problem and have you noticed

everyone in their cars with their windows
proudly rolled all the way down
listens to the radio into the day

always with a male voice shouting the problem
inside the solution everyone said
was a plan we were warned would not work right away

was not caused by something we did
but we seem right away to have forgotten
and now we have a right

to be angry a right to our collective anger
this is what people say others talk
about old days everyone lived

on a hill before we were wounded they say
we don't know what we want
I want to go to sleep again and wake

somewhere and turn on the faucet
without feeling as if I am destroying anything
and drink some coffee that doesn't taste like blood

o you can try to be a peaceful shadow
you can but you never will be
you are not past all argument this is not

one of those movies that starts
with blue painted steps and ends
with everything meaning something definite

you can't quite say but you leave the theater
knowing for a little while open your heart
doesn't mean anything the heart is not a door

Poem for Russia with a White Plastic Wolf

Dear Russian people
I am standing
like some retired general
above the wooden kitchen table
looking down on an actual
map of the world.
The red teapot rattles
and the radio worries
about the fate
of a hundred whales.
Everyone wants
you to send a ship
to blow up the ice
they wandered into
probably never thinking
it would not be water.
As always the experts
say it's bad to let
short term sadness decide.
Down I look
on massive Alaska.
Like the head
of a gentle white
snow beast facing
left it is always
across the blue strait
known as Bering
about to ceremoniously
kiss its mother.
I like the way

the dotted line
separating our night
from yours comes
straight down then slides
to the right to pass
through the narrows.
I place my finger
on Tin City
then abandoned Naukan
where Eskimo lived
in the time
before us or you
and then I push
my pointer finger
with its pearl
nail like a cosmonaut
breathing behind
a face mask farther
westward over Siberia
and the Sea of Okhotsk
toward Baikal older
than any thought
then over to empty
Dead Lake
Cheybek-Kohl
where no fish swim
high in the old
mountain place.
Last night
at the top
of a glass hotel I drank
much amazing wine.

Thankfully no one
asked what I do.
Though it is summer
this morning is cold.
The electric heater
makes a rasping sound.
A truck goes by
shaking the table
and the tiny
white plastic wolf
I placed on the map
in California.
Its feet point west
like it is ready
into the future to leap.
Away from the Pacific
it turns its head
back to the east
and our capital
over an uncertain shoulder.

Albert Einstein

only a few people
really try to understand
relativity like my father
who for decades kept
the same gray book
next to his bed
with diagrams
of arrows connecting
clocks and towers
in the morning
he'd cook eggs
and holding
a small red saucepan
tell us his tired children
a radio on a train
passing at light speed
could theoretically
play tomorrow's songs
now he is gone
yes it's confusing
I have placed
my plastic plant
in front of the window
its eternal leaves
sip false peace
my worldly nature
comforts me
I wish we had
a radio sunlight
powers so without

wasting precious
electrons we could listen
to news concerning
Africa's southern coast
where people with giant
colored sails
are trying to harness
the cool summer wind
with its special name
I always forget
last night I read a book
which said he was born
an old determinist
and clearly it was all
beautiful guesses
and I watched you knowing
where you travel
when you sleep
I will never know

Ode to Fluffy

goodbye Fluffy
we hardly knew you
you were here
just a few
ordinary weeks
on your way
from a feral life
to a new home
with an ancient woman
whose husband died
on the couch
she waited
you never arrived
it sounds absurd
to say it hurts
we will miss
your gray eyes
the color of nothing
from this world
you were wild
and happy to be
for a time
that turned out
to be the end
resting with us
the ones who gather
in the morning
in the kitchen
to ritually hold
the milk and argue

it came amid

the usual commotion

we all heard

what you said

we never knew

what it meant

you had a pain

we couldn't help

you were destined

for the earth

in the backyard

a solemn moment

playing silent

music all around us

Your Story

dear old friend
are you angry
why won't you write me
beloved teacher
is what I called you
in my mind
mild morning
California depressing light
uncertainly standing
between the rooms
I ask myself
why such anger
I walk downtown
busy worrying
all day I feel
I am sure
a man is holding
an important geranium
in a story
you are writing
the geranium
I see
is golden
there is no such thing
as a gold geranium
except on the ear
who would wear
such horrible jewelry
it is also a color
deep zonal scarlet

I had a couch
it was totally red
I gave it to Betsy
her gray cat sleeps
she is in her garden
confusingly most geraniums
are not
they are some other flower
genus pelargonium
who cares
eventually everyone

Poem for Lu Chi

All day it has wanted to rain.
A constant breeze
from the north where shadows live
in ancient government
among the old huge trees
carries a little scent of wood
into the city. It ruffles
some waxy green leaves
outside my window
in this office building.
The window is very solid,
my hair is completely still.
Lu Chi, in the third century
you wrote your treatise
to discover the difference
between good and bad writing.
But you already knew
the leaves fall in autumn
and each artist has
a particular way
to magic and sadness.
I know my beloved
is very close, she works
down the street
in a modern building
made of orange neon and steel,
I don't have to dream of her,
she is very far away from heaven,
there are no actual mountains
between us. Soon we will

have lunch together.
Then maybe I will write
a letter and drop it
into a blue box. Some rivers
go underground, I know
one here in the city
beneath the armory
flows, many times
I have walked above it
and felt a peace I am happy
I will never be able to explain.

Poem for a Vial of Nameless Perfume

Finally stranger at the end of a long season
of constant beginnings I opened at last
the letter containing tissue paper
so carefully folded around the vial you sent me.
With giant fingers I unscrewed the black
cap marveling at such jeweled industry.
The clear liquid smelled at first
like a vast tiny ballroom full of hopes
someone else's mother had
rubbing one wrist against another
in that manner reserved for distracted
excited ready to be disappointed realists
who know for a moment all dreams matter.
I bent my head to the glass jar
and knew it was the same scent worn
by the woman staring out
of the gilded framed canvas at me
yesterday at the modern museum.
She was lying on a red realistic
yet also somehow along the edges
disintegrating couch. She must have been
at the very last party before painters
discovered abstraction and started painting
the multicolored edge of this wondrous
contaminated storm cloud age we find
ourselves alone together drinking
so much information from,
while the keepers of the house
we have not elected discuss just war
and our server farms sound like the ultimate

bee colony touching ceremoniously
down on a field of magenta flowers.
And now the third and therefore
most holy time I bring it to my face,
searching for some actual connection
to any unsentient genus my nose
could bring my brain, but there
was nothing, no gentle stroke
of the orphan forehead, no memory
of summer walking along the beach
still holding a few dried crumbling
leaves from the fragrant grove,
only the thought because I am actually
on a typewriter typing on a ghostly
anachronistic piece of paper
I will physically send you
to truly hold, a few molecules
once part of me to your ceiling
or who knows if we are both lucky
skylight will rise, and then
an electric wheelchair through
the green space inside you
from now on everyone will know
as Emerald Park will quietly carry
a dreaming young soldier,
the room will get sadder, you will be
on an island with very long night
approaching and clouds will pass
over your head and no one will ever
know what they resembled.

Poem for Jack Spicer

It's the start of baseball season,
and I am thinking again
as I do every year
in early April now
that I live in California
where afternoon is a blue
span to languidly cross
of those long ones
you used to sort of sleep
through getting drunk
on many beers, lying
next to your radio
on a little square of grass
in the sun, listening
half to the game and half
to the Pacific water gently
slapping the concrete
barrier of the man-made cove.
I have heard it and it sounds
like conversations among
not there people I can't
quite hear. But you could.
And later you would try
to remember what they said
and transcribe it on your
black typewriter
in your sad, horrible room.
When I read your poems
about suicide and psychoanalysis
I feel very lucky and ashamed

to be alive at all. Everyone
has been talking lately
about radiation, iodine,
and wind, and you are in
your grave, far from the water.
I know I don't care about you
at all but when I look
at your photograph,
your round head tilted up
so you are staring down
at everyone, I remember
how much you hated your body.
Today I will go down by the water
where you used to sit and think
I do not hate my body
even though I often do.
When I die please write he tried
on whatever stone you choose.

Poem for Bill Cassidy

I wish I would
like a ship
that all night carries
its beloved captain
sleeping through
no weather
slip past dawn
and wake with nothing
to report
but strange things
that did not happen
but I get up
in the dark
and parachute
quietly down
to the kitchen
to begin
the purely mental
ritual plugging
in of the useless
worry machine
above me
she sleeps
like the innocent
still dreaming older
sister to all
gentle things
the white screen
impassively asks
me to say what

does not matter
does so I shut
it down and think
about the lake
near where I live
it's a lagoon
getting lighter
like an old blue
just switched on
television
maybe a Zenith
it has two arms
they stretch
without feeling
east to embrace
an empty park
a little light
then everything
has a shadow
I almost hear
a silent bell
low voices
brought us
to this old city
the port connects
to the world
where everyone
pretends to know
they live
on an island
waiting for
the giant wave

in some form
maybe radiation
in the yard
the wind blows
the whole black
sky looks down
for an instant
through my sleepy
isolate frame
a complex child
hologram flickers
angrily holding
a green plastic shovel
then disappears
leaving an empty
column waiting
Bill who I knew
was so angry
is dead
whatever he was
going through
I kept away
I never did
anything
I love his poem
he was really good
I keep forgetting
his last name
I always leave
his handmade book
on my desk
not to remember

but because for hours
after everything
everyone says
sounds like a language
I never knew
but now speak
spirit I know
you would have hated
how I think
you would have liked
this music
in another room
pushing the alien
voice into
the millennium
the one you left
so early
spirit
you were right
all noble
things are gone
except to struggle
and be loved

Telegraph Flowers

I stood a while
before the flowers
I always passed
on my way
to wherever
I was going,
for once this time
just touching
those white plastic
tabs someone
had so carefully
held a black
sharpie and written
Latin and familiar
names onto.
It always seemed
this flower shop
had interposed
its fragile green
plants and every
colored blossoms
between the store
full of books
and the famous
chaotic street
whose name
means message
that crosses far.
Sometimes the message
says come here

from everywhere,
the revolution
dream has filled
the people again,
soon they will go
and maybe too simply
say what they feel
to the covered
faces of the beneath
their helmets totally
human riot police.
And sometimes
you private being
I am a river
pouring books
and people talking
into the great
plaza inside you.
The bookstore
was closing forever.
Past me people
walked like it was
for something
not time
but it was
it was the last day
I could ever pass
through the doors
and take down
volumes from shelves
I stood before
when I was a student

of what I thought
I should be
a student of.
Then I tried
to fill my head
but now I know
it has a socket
and like a plastic
globe light cover
surrounding
an indicator
light it lights
up only when
I converse
with the dead.
I stood
before the doors.
On the street
dogs and people.
I hoped on them
a little money
and no rain
would fall.
My breath
without me
traveled in
to say
nothing
to the books
soon by time
and hands to be
dispersed.

Most will never
if they ever
were be read again.
I know things
are more important,
so I bought a plant
and held it
while I listened
to the woman
slowly give me
careful instructions.
I think she said
my son
if you do
one thing wherever
you find yourself
just be celestial,
that is light
in reflection
and also heavy
for you have returned
where you belong.

Poem for California

when she leaves
for work I feel
I have forgotten
something but still
remember the way
to the lake
in Minnesota
where one very
cold night
many years ago
I fell and snapped
the anklebone
every night
for weeks I walked
with someone else
our skates thrown
over our shoulders
were we pretending
to be kids? I still
wasn't sure I resided
anywhere in particular
the very cold city
with its chain
of peaceable water
bodies moving
past brick mill
buildings filled
with harmless
commerce and light
industry had

in its own way
welcomed me
though I was still
not finished
saying goodbye
to everything
later that spring
after the operation
for most of the day
she was at work
it seemed okay
I didn't understand
the process healing
my broken ankle
those long afternoons
I limped through
the neighborhood
we lived near a museum
it was always quiet
early one evening
she said the radio
was haunted
I was pouring wine
my hand was shaking
like it has for years
I didn't want to know
anything at all
now all that matters
in California
is how this feeling
can be useful
some dark anger

lives in the trees
I want to see it
I swivel my head
very hungry
to see what everyone's
life is like
maybe an owl
it took me two tries
to move all my shit
to California
it's a big country
have you been?
it's actually
at least two states
north is terribly
lonely green
hills and also yellow
grasses with blue
water glimpses
when you get closer
the Pacific is not
peaceful at all
little towns are
peaceful that is
surrounded by ancient
trees that even
if you are not spiritual
seem to listen
even I with my tiny
black heart am changed
if you come visit
it will be awkward

I'll make some chili
Sarah will be nice
last night I dreamed
my scar was pulsing
when I woke
this morning it hurt
I can't believe
that's my only problem

American Singer

in memory of Vic Chesnutt

when I walk
to the mailbox
holding the letter
that fails to say
how sorry I am
you feel your call
or any words at all
on that day
would have stopped
the great singer
who long ago
decided more
quickly through
to move
I notice probably
because you wrote
that strange
word *funeral*
the constant black
fabric I think
is taffeta
always draped
over the scaffolds
the figures
scraping paint
are wearing dusty
protective suits
and to each other

saying nothing
I move invisibly
like a breeze
around three men
wearing advanced
practically weightless
jackets impervious
to all possible
weather even
a hurricane
I hear them say
something German
then photograph
the pale blue
turrets that floating
up in fog
seem noble
heads full
of important thoughts
like what revolution
could make us happy
from some window
wandering horns
he was three
when I was born
for a long time
I had no ideas
my father worked
in a private office
full of quiet
people working
I came to visit

it seemed correct
I went to college
studied things
dyed my hair
felt a rage
disguised as love
kept escaping
suffering only
a few broken bones
everything healed
now I live
in California
where in some
red and golden
theater I saw
him howl
such unfathomable
force from only
one lung
it was one
of his last shows
in Athens once
many years
ago we shared
a cigarette
a little smoke
from our faces
I can't remember
so many things
but see him
in his wheelchair
his folded body

it's all gone
but for electrons
I can still push
into my ears
I choose the song
the perfect one
hear his words
and see
the mirror
in the ancient
lighthouse blinking
brave ships
somehow
you crossed
the water carrying
what we need
you can rest
light as nothing
in the harbor
we will take it
and go on

About the Author

Matthew Zapruder is the author of four collections of poetry. He is also cotranslator of *Secret Weapon,* the final collection by the late Romanian poet Eugen Jebeleanu. The recipient of a 2011 Guggenheim Fellowship, he is an editor at Wave Books and an assistant professor in the Department of English and the MFA in Creative Writing at St. Mary's College of California. He lives in Oakland.

Poetry is vital to language and living. Since 1972, Copper Canyon Press has published extraordinary poetry from around the world to engage the imaginations and intellects of readers, writers, booksellers, librarians, teachers, students, and donors.

WE ARE GRATEFUL FOR THE MAJOR SUPPORT PROVIDED BY:

THE PAUL G. ALLEN
FAMILY FOUNDATION

amazon.com

the
POINT
WHERE LESS IS MORE

golden
lasso

Lannan

THE MAURER FAMILY
FOUNDATION

NATIONAL
ENDOWMENT
FOR THE ARTS

WASHINGTON STATE
ARTS COMMISSION

Anonymous
Arcadia Fund
John Branch
Diana and Jay Broze
Beroz Ferrell & The Point, llc
Janet and Les Cox
Mimi Gardner Gates
Gull Industries, Inc.
on behalf of William and Ruth True
Mark Hamilton and Suzie Rapp
Carolyn and Robert Hedin
Steven Myron Holl
Lakeside Industries, Inc.
on behalf of Jeanne Marie Lee
Maureen Lee and Mark Busto
Brice Marden
New Mexico Community Foundation
H. Stewart Parker
Penny and Jerry Peabody
John Phillips and Anne O'Donnell
Joseph C. Roberts
Cynthia Lovelace Sears and Frank Buxton
The Seattle Foundation
Dan Waggoner
Charles and Barbara Wright
The dedicated interns and faithful
volunteers of Copper Canyon Press

To learn more about underwriting Copper Canyon Press titles,
please call 360-385-4925 ext. 103

The Chinese character for poetry is made up of two parts:
"word" and "temple." It also serves as pressmark for
Copper Canyon Press.

The poems are set in Minion with headings in Gill Sans Condensed.
Book design and composition by Phil Kovacevich.